Leaks, WikiLeaks and the Press

Leaks, WikiLeaks and the Press

Did the India-US-UK & Russia-US-UK Bilateral Relations Influence Iraq War Leaks Coverage by Indian and Russian Press?

Shamim Zakaria

ISBN- 9781723921100

About the Author

Shamim Zakaria is journalist, author and academic. Born and brought-up in India's northeast, he did his schooling and spent most part of his early life in Guwahati before relocating to Delhi to pursue graduate study and thereafter to England for post-graduation. He holds a bachelor's degree with honors in Journalism and Mass Communication from India and a master's degree in International Journalism from the University of Sussex, United Kingdom. His writings are focused primarily on politics, human rights and other socio-political issues. His multitudinous articles have found place in a plethora of regional, national and international publications, disseminating in print and online. He has lived and worked internationally based out of India, England and China.

Leaks, WikiLeaks and the Press was initially an academic essay written during his post graduate study, which is now published as a book.

He has previously authored **India's Invisible Shackles** which is available online for purchase.

Visit his website:
www.shamimzakaria.com

Get in touch:
mail@shamimzakaria.com

Join him on social media:
www.facebook.com/shamimzakariaofficial
www.twitter.com/shamimzakaria
www.instagram.com/shamim.zakaria

Leaks, WikiLeaks and the Press

Did India-US-UK & Russia-US-UK Bilateral Relations Influence Iraq War Leaks Coverage by Indian and Russian Press?

Shamim Zakaria

Leaks, WikiLeaks and the Press

Shamim Zakaria

Table of Contents

Introduction-

This book is an analysis of how the Iraq War leaks published by WikiLeaks was reported by the press in Russia and India in-terms of the relationship both these countries share with the United States and the United Kingdom. It further analyses if diplomatic relations had any impact on the content of reportage.

It begins by giving a brief explanation of what is WikiLeaks, then it goes on to put forward snippets of the 2003 Iraq invasion and how the event was portrayed by the media in India and Russia. Thereafter, light has been thrown on the India-UK-US and Russia-UK-US relations, finally followed by an analysis of the news coverage. While looking at the diplomatic relations, the past terms and the present scenario of the bilateral relations has also been looked upon.

For the purpose of analysis only stories appearing in newspaper and news portals are being scrutinized. Both while looking at the coverage of 2003 Iraq invasion and Iraq war leaks, a total of three news stories appearing in three different newspapers/portals has been analyzed.

Also, columns and articles penned by political analysts has been looked upon to get a wider purview of the bilateral relations of the countries.

Shamim Zakaria

WikiLeaks: A backgrounder

As explained by the authors in Beyond WikiLeaks, 'WikiLeaks' was founded in 2006 as an online platform for whistle-blowers and for publishing information that is censored by public authorities and private actors (Brevini, Patrick, 2). The goals of WikiLeaks has been defined as to harness the speed, interactivity, and global reach of the internet to provide a fast and secure mechanism to anonymously submit information, and to make that information accessible to a global audience (Beyond WikiLeaks, 2013). The authors in Beyond WikiLeaks further inform that in its first few years of existence, WikiLeaks electronically published a range of documents of varying significance that had mixed media impact (Brevini, Patrick, 3)

As per the official website of WikiLeaks this is how they elicit their functioning (wilileaks.org)

'Our goal is to bring important news and information to the public. We provide an innovative, secure and anonymous way for sources to leak information to our journalists. One of our most important activities is to publish original source material alongside our news stories so readers and historians alike can see evidence of the truth. We are a young organisation that has grown very quickly, relying on a network of dedicated volunteers around the globe. Since 2007, when the organisation was officially launched, WikiLeaks has worked to report on and publish important information. We also develop and adapt technologies to support these activities' (Wikileaks.org, 2015).

Mentioning about the anonymity of its sources the official website states that WikiLeaks has never revealed its sources, thus implying that safety and anonymity of informants is of prime importance for the organization (2015).

It goes on to say:

What we can say is that we operate a number of servers across multiple international jurisdictions and we do not keep logs. Hence these logs cannot be seized. Anonymization occurs early in the WikiLeaks network, long before information passes to our web servers. Without specialized global internet traffic analysis, multiple parts of our organisation must conspire with each other to strip submitters of their anonymity' (wikileaks.org, 2015).

A part in the 'about' section of WikiLeaks also finds mention of the awards the website has been conferred with. Some of them include the 2008 Economist Index on Censorship Freedom of Expression award; the 2009 Amnesty International human rights reporting award (New Media).

The authenticity of every story is also testified before it is published in the website and they assess all news stories and test their veracity (Wikileaks.org, 2015).

And as per the founders this is how the website vouches for authentic content:

We send a submitted document through a very detailed examination and procedure. Is it real? What elements prove it is real? Who would have the motive to fake such a document and why? We use traditional investigative journalism techniques as well as more modern technology-based methods. Typically, we will do a forensic analysis of the document, determine the cost of forgery, means, motive, opportunity, the claims of the apparent authoring organisation, and answer a set of other detailed questions about the document' (wikileaks.org, 2015)

2003:US Invasion of Iraq

Bassam Romaya in 'The Iraq War a philosophical analysis' has termed the Iraq invasion as one of the most controversial international conflict of recent times thus arguments about the various sides of the war, the ethical and moral aspect continues till date (Romaya, 2). Eliciting about the unfolding of events of the war Romaya informs the war was formally inaugurated by the United States on March 19, 2003. Three weeks into the invasion, the conflict was transformed into a military occupation, shortly after the overthrow of the Iraqi Ba'ath Party (Romaya, 3).

According to the view of the American government and their allies, as a legitimate, defensive response to the threat of weapons of mass destruction (WMD), which the Saddam Hussein government allegedly had in its arsenal (Danju, Maasoglu, 682). The journal 'The Reasons Behind U.S. Invasion Of Iraq' explaining further about the arguments of the war says, Saddam Hussein's government was immediately perceived as a threat and an affront to the international community in the wake of the September 11, 2001 bombing of the world trade centre (Danju, Maasoglu, 682). America has found a casus belli to go to war under the so-called 'war on terrorism' slogan (Danju, Maasoglu, 682). What the United States of America alleged was there had been a strong linkage between Saddam Hussein and international terrorism and the first priority of the United States government is to protect its citizens and its political and economic interests; its national security is always paramount (Romaya, 5).

Also, what political argument Danju and Maasoglu gave was, the United States significantly supports democratic governments around the world and the Baathist regime was seen as totalitarian and undemocratic thus consequently, regime change in Iraq became the U.S. priority and the only way to achieve that was through the use of force (The Reasons Behind U.S. Invasion of Iraq, 682). Therefore, the Iraqi regime was a threat to the national security of America, and America and its allies had to launch a pre-emptive strike at the heart of the Baathist outfit and remove the existential threat that it represented to America and the free world (Danju,Maasoglu,683).

After nearly a decade of relentless battle the 'Status of Forces Agreement' between the Iraqi government and the United States that was approved in December 2008 concluded that the combat forces must withdraw by 30 June, 2009 and the remaining US forces must be out of Iraq by December 31, 2011 (Romaya, 2). The dates were provisionally set according to the security scenario of that particular period (Romaya, 2).

Shamim Zakaria

US Invasion of Iraq in Indian and Russian Press

The Iraq invasion by US received an extensive coverage by news media all across the globe. Similarly, it has continued to throng the Indian and Russian media as well. Contemplating, particularly the coverage in the print media, following could be discerned.

In one of the news reports featured in the newswire Indo-Asian News Service (IANS) the headline stated that former Australian prime minister John Howard was embarrassed about the deployment of troops in the 2003 US-led invasion to oust Iraqi dictator Saddam Hussein (IANS, 2014). The article further stated the reason of that is 'existence of weapons of mass destruction (WMD) as a mere excuse for the war and goes on to say that even after more than a decade of the conflict, no proof has ever been found of a WMD arsenal in Iraq (IANS, 2014).

The Kashmir Monitor newspaper in one of its articles called the reasons behind waging the war as a fiction (2011). It further mentioned about non existence of any proof of WMD, simply because the weapons themselves did not exist in any shape or form (Kashmir Monitor, 2011).

Another Indian newspaper, The Times of India went on to quote and emphasise on the number of deaths in the very first paragraph of one of its articles further eliciting the ramifications of the US invasion of Iraq (2014). This news report, for depicting the disapproval of common people of the war, mentioned about a website arrestblair.org that offered a bounty of £2,150 to anyone who could arrest the erstwhile Prime minister of Britain, Tony Blair for crimes against peace (The Times of India, 2014).

Throwing light on the coverage of US invasion of Iraq in Russia, a story appearing in The Moscow Times in its very first line begins by stating, 'flip through Russian newspapers or surf the television channels and one thing becomes clear: no one supports the U.S.-led coalition in Iraq' (2003). The report further criticises the Bush administration for its disregard of international law and order, and goes on to selectively quote voices who have criticised the war. Meanwhile state-owned Russia television's "Vesti" program having a banner over the war coverage on its website reading simply "U.S. Aggression", also found mention on the report (The Moscow Times, 2003).

This news report also quoted Alexei Pankin, editor of the Sreda media journal who said, "Everybody wants this war to be over quickly, and it is clear that America will win. But everybody wants America to be dealt as many blows in the face as possible. There is a feeling of surprising satisfaction with the fact that the U.S. military machine hasn't turned out to be as mighty as advertised" (The Moscow Times, 2003).

The news story however provided a one liner quote of the then chief editor of BBC Russian Service's Moscow bureau, Konstantin Eggert, who mentioned there's no reporter who fully supports the war (2003). However, this quote of Konstantin Eggert was written in an indirect speech and was placed towards the end of article.

As of recently while reporting the recent interview of former Prime Minister of Britain, Tony Blair where he said supporting the US led invasion of Iraq a mistake, the Moscow News published it under the headline-'Britain's Blair says 2003 Iraq invasion played role in Islamic State rise' (2015). The news primarily focused on how it was the 2003 invasion of Iraq which led to the rise of Islamic State. The report in the Moscow News also mentions about certain unnamed critics who according to this newspaper believes that, 'US decision to disband Saddam Hussein's army after the invasion created a huge security vacuum exploited by al Qaeda, which was eventually replaced by Islamic State' (Moscow News, 2015).

Again quoting anonymous former Iraqi army officers, members of the Sunni Muslim minority this news story goes on to claim that, Shi'ite-led government backed by Western powers, are senior strategists in Islamic State (2015). The topic of Islamic State thronged major content of the news but only at the end this story quoted Tony Blair who said, "I find it hard to apologise for removing Saddam. I think, even from today in 2015, it is better that he's not there than that he is there" (Moscow News, 2015).

Iraq War Leaks in a Capsule

On 22nd October 2010, WikiLeaks released apparently one of the biggest classified military leaks of war in history till date. As stated in the WikiLeaks website it leaked 391,832 reports titled as 'The Iraq War Logs' which document the war and occupation in Iraq. The data stretches from 1st January 2004 to 31st December 2009 (except for the months of May 2004 and March 2009) as told by soldiers in the United States Army(WikiLeaks.org,2010). The official WikiLeaks website states the following on the content of the leaks:

'The reports detail 109,032 deaths in Iraq, comprised of 66,081 'civilians'; 23,984 'enemy' (those labelled as insurgents); 15,196 'host nation' (Iraqi government forces) and 3,771 'friendly' (coalition forces). The majority of the deaths (66,000, over 60%) of these are civilian deaths. That is 31 civilians dying every day during the six-year period. For comparison, the 'Afghan War Diaries', previously released by WikiLeaks, covering the same period, detail the deaths of some 20,000 people. Iraq during the same period, was five times as lethal with equivalent population size.' (WikiLeaks, 2010).

According to reports published in newspaper The Guardian, leaked data had details of more than 100,000 people killed in Iraq following the US-led invasion, including more than 15,000 deaths that were previously unrecorded. (2010)

The report titled 'Iraq War Logs Reveal 15,000 Previously Unlisted Civilian Deaths' quoted the following startling figures (The Guardian, 2010)-

The logs record a total of 109,032 violent deaths between 2004 and 2009. It is claimed that 66,081 of these were civilians. A further 23,984 deaths are classed as 'enemy' and 15,196 as members of the Iraqi security forces. The logs also include the deaths of 3,771 US and allied soldiers. No fewer than 31,780 of the total deaths are attributed to the improvised landmines laid around Iraq by insurgents. There were 65,439 successful improvised explosive device (IED) blasts in the period, according to the logs, with another 44,620 IEDs found in time and disarmed' (The Guardian, 2010).

However, the Iraq Body Count (IBQ), which was a London-based group that monitors civilian casualties gave a contradicting view. According to IBQ the data leaked by WikiLeaks cannot be vouched for (2010). A statement of IBC quoted in a The Guardian news story (2010) said the following:

'The data (of WikiLeaks) cannot be relied upon as a complete record of Iraqi deaths. IBC, for example, had previously calculated that up to 91,469 civilians were killed from various causes during the period covered by the leaked database. While detailing the 15,000 previously unknown deaths, it also omits many otherwise well-attested civilian fatalities caused by US troops themselves. Nor does the Pentagon data cover any of the initial invasion fighting throughout 2003; IBC has identified 12,080 purely civilian deaths in that year' (The Guardian, 2010).

Indo-US Ties

India's relationship with the United States has always been like a mixed pickle. During almost 10 years of Dr. Manmohan Singh-led United Progressive Alliance (UPA) government, India's relations with the US held all the promises of becoming robust and a model strategic partnership for international relations (Mahapatra, 170).

The writer (Mahapatra, 170) also mentions the Indo-US nuclear deal as historic and a stepping stone in bilateral relations between both the countries. He goes on to say that a large number of defence deals, including arms trade and technology transfer, the conclusion of a new 10-year defence framework agreement, regular military exercises involving all branches of the armed forces and efforts towards enhancing bilateral trade and investment ties were remarkable developments in bilateral relations (Mahapatra, 170).

Obama administration's term coincided with two Indian Prime ministers, Dr. Manmohan Singh of UPA and the present Prime minister Narendra Modi of the Bharatiya Janata Party (BJP). After the change of guards in White House with Barack Obama taking charge as US President, questions were raised about the continuity of Bush's policy towards India, but President Obama didn't disappoint any of the Prime ministers (Mahapatra, 171).

Firstly, during his visit to Delhi in 2010 Obama announced his support for India's permanent membership in the UN Security Council, Missile Technology Control Regime (MCTR), Nuclear Suppliers' Group (NSG) and other non-proliferation regimes (Mahapatra, 171).

Also during the time of 2014 Indian general elections when, Narendra Modi was foreseen as the plausible Indian Prime minister, the first action the US initiated was revamping its relations (Mahapatra, 171). Things began by the US revoking the visa ban it had put on Modi in 2005, for his alleged role in a 2002 communal riots in India. While revoking the ban it was pointed out that the head of a state would not require a visa to enter the US (Mahapatra, 172). In the meanwhile, the arrest of an Indian female consular officer and her perceived mistreatment on December 11, 2013, by the New York Police Department (NYPD) created a diplomatic furore, the goal of a robust Indo-US strategic partnership seemed to have entered rough waters (Mahapatra, 171). But, apart for drawing unusual media attention against the backdrop of the rocky political ties over her arrest, it couldn't impede the ties (Mahapatra, 172).

Furthermore, Prime minister Modi's recent visit to the United States in 2014 as the new PM of India was seen as a momentous development both in terms of unprecedented methods and new initiatives to reshape and invigorate the bilateral strategic partnership (Mahapatra, 173).

Indo-UK Ties

Rob Lynes the director of British Council in India believes that the UK-India relationship is strong, with a shared history going back centuries, and now a shared vision of the future (BBC, 2015). He further elicits that since 2010 UK Prime Minister David Cameron has visited India three times, and the UK diplomatic network in India is now the largest in the world (BBC, 2015).

According to a BBC article the UK and India have more than 200 years of shared history, strong democracies, connected cultural institutions and the English language (2015). Further the piece states that the Indian diaspora, which totals about 1.5 million people and is the largest ethnic minority group in the UK, has a very important role to play in helping to strengthen the links between the two countries (BBC, 2015). The article goes on to say, "It is the seventh greatest Indian diaspora in the world and is well represented across all walks of life in the UK. The achievements cross everything from business to sport, and science and politics" (BBC, 2015).

Throwing light on the upcoming generation of the country, young Indians still believe they have a good understanding of the UK and thus are attracted to the country (Emer Lotten Dubber, 18). The authors of the report say that young middle-class Indians were asked to rank the overall attractiveness of the 15 biggest economies, and the UK came second, behind the US (Emer Lotten Dubber, 20).

However, there also seems to be contradicting views as well. According to an article published in Independent, ignorance of India among young Britons risks jeopardising the special relationship between the two countries, and could see Britain losing out as a result (2015).

While suggesting that Britain needs to act swiftly to strengthen its relationship with India, the article states that the number of Indian students choosing to study in Britain has dropped with rapid pace in the past five years (Independent, 2015). Furthermore, according to this very same news article the UK has gone from being one of India's top trading partners in 1999 to 18th in 2015 (Independent, 2015).

However, the recent visit of the Indian Prime Minister, Mr. Narendra Modi which is the first after a decade is seen having a great significance rejuvenating diplomatic relation of both the countries (Rowlatt, 2015).

Coverage by Indian Press

Now shifting focus back to the coverage of Iraq War logs, the leaks by WikiLeaks created a hullabaloo around the globe and was covered by the global media. Espying how it was covered in India, English daily Hindustan times carried a detailed report explaining Iraq war leaks and various data associated with it. The report in its very first sentence termed WikiLeaks as a 'whistle-blowing' organisation stating, 'whistle-blowing website WikiLeaks on Friday released nearly 400,000 classified US military files chronicling the Iraq war from 2004 through 2009, the largest leak of its kind in US military history……' (The Hindustan Times, 2010). Further by the use of adjective 'largest' it automatically portrayed US military in the losing end. This report by Hindustan Times also under various subheadings like 'prisoner abuse' and 'civilian deaths' highlighted the data further making the report gripping and intriguing for the readers (2010).

The Times of India (TOI) few weeks after the leaks that created enough noise globally, published a 968-word report entirely based on Jullian Assange's article titled, 'Don't shoot messenger for revealing uncomfortable truths,' that he wrote on December 8, 2010. The news report by TOI headlined- 'Don't shoot the messenger: Assange,' was entirely based on Assange's quotes extracted from his article. The news story termed Assange's leaks and the consequent arrest by Australian authorities as 'passionate espousal of freedom of speech' (The Times of India, 2010).

The news story seemingly picked up audacious extracts from Assange's article and reported them with opening sentences like '….stressing that democratic societies need a strong media' and 'powers of the Australian government appear to be fully at the disposal of the US' (The Times of India, 2010). The TOI news report also calls the hounding of Jullian Assange as 'vicious attacks and accusations from the US government and its followers' (2010).

Kashmir Observer another national daily was seen reporting the event of Iraq war logs with the use of an utter strong language. It published a news story under the headline 'Hidden World of US Diplomacy Exposed' (2010). The story portrayed US being at the receiving end by stating 'United States was catapulted into a worldwide diplomatic crisis' in the very first line of the news story (Kashmir Observer, 2010). The news piece by Kashmir Observer stated that The Pentagon is 'infuriated' by WikiLeaks leaked files (2010). Furthermore, the news story while quoting Jullian Assange's clarification termed the leaks a serving 'important public interest' (Kashmir Observer, 2010).

However, a different line of reporting was seen on part of the newspaper Mail Today. A news story published in December, 2010 that reported on the turf between Jullian Assange and WikiLeaks' former spokesperson Daniel Domscheit- Berg, was seen to be critical of Assange and the Iraq War leaks. Using quotes of Domscheit, Mail Today maintained that Assange's decision to leak the Afghan diaries and Iraq War logs led to a disarray within the whistle-blower site (2010). Mail Today in this same story also put emphasis on the growing dissent within Wikileaks and informed that Herbert Snorrason, a 25- year- old student from Iceland who had volunteered with the site, was shown the door for questioning Domscheit- Berg's suspension (2010).

Mail Today's critical approach towards WikiLeaks could be linked with the newspaper's association with the British newspaper Daily Mail (Live Mint, 2007). Mail Today which was launched on 2007 is published by the India Today Group but British newspaper Daily Mail owns a 26% stake which it bought at ₹180 million (The Hindu, 2007).

Russia-US Ties

Russia has maintained a disturbed relationship with the US since long. Also, since the Soviet collapse, Russia has been an issue in every US presidential election campaign (Stent, 123). As one writer further puts, the US–Russia relationship emerged as a contentious issue in the run-up to Putin's re-election as president; in fact, it loomed considerably larger in Russia than in the United States (Stent, 124). Anti-Americanism became a central theme of Putin's campaign in reaction to the rise of an unexpected opposition protest movement after the contested December 2011 Duma elections; the movement continued during and after the March presidential elections (Stent, 124).

Though even after two decades the tone of the Cold War is often invoked, Russia no longer represents the bilateral foreign-policy preoccupation for US policymakers that the USSR once did (Stent, 125). Nevertheless, Russia's geostrategic position as the world's largest continental power, its nuclear-weapons arsenal and its permanent seat on the UN Security Council will ensure that it remains a key partner for the United States (Stent, 125).

Further, Russia remains an important interlocutor for the United States as the consequences of the Arab Spring play themselves out and as the question of Iran's nuclear programme continues to unfold (Stent, 136). Russia will remain an important US partner, albeit a challenging (Stent, 136). It is unlikely that there will be another reset in US–Russian relations in the foreseeable future (Stent, 135).

Shamim Zakaria

Russia-UK Ties

Though the European Union has proved to be a significant forum for managing relations with Russia. The same cannot be said for the UK (David, 201). In successive foreign policy documents, the EU is referenced as just one of a wider circle of arrangements through which the UK's relations with Russia are conducted (David, 201).

It's been argued that though neither UK nor Russia is necessarily reliant upon each other but common threats and challenges and the desire to trade mean neither is entirely independent of the other either, however an intervening and often detrimental variable in this is the USA (David, 202). It is believed that when Russian prime minister Putin visited Britain in 2003 an attempt supposedly was chalked out to re-establish good relations between UK and Russia, however until then it was widely understood that Russia had found more harmony in Paris and Berlin (David, 204). According to diplomatic experts the relationship between UK and Russia soured as after Britain's support to the Iraq War of 2003 (David, 205).

Putting light on the present scenario in a recent article by Matt Dathan, the political reporter of Independent wrote that the gruesome Paris attack and a subsequent might trigger a revival of UK-Russian relations (2015). The report further quoted President Putin thanking David Cameron for sharing intelligence about the Sinai plane crash at G20 summit in Turkey where Putin humbly accepted that relations between the two countries are not of the best (Independent, 2015).

Coverage by Russian Press

In an article published in The Moscow Times the Iraq war leaks were termed as an interesting read as it exposes the fatal policies of the United States (2010). The piece goes on to exhort Jullian Assange as someone driven by a noble principle, 'even though he is wanted in Sweden to face rape, sexual molestation and unlawful coercion charges, was driven by one noble principle — that good should prevail over evil' (The Moscow Times, 2010).

However, as the write-up proceeds the author adopted a different line by claiming that Assange's leaks make it easier for the Taliban to capture, torture and kill the secret informants in Afghanistan who are working for the U.S. military (The Moscow Times, 2010). And the author mocks him by stating, al-Qaida counterintelligence should bestow Assange with the Bin Laden Award for outstanding service in the fight against U.S. infidels (The Moscow Times, 2010).

Another news story appearing in The Moscow Times, stated that the leaks have revealed a hidden world of backstage international diplomacy (2010). Also the news story had put the statement of Whitehouse only towards the end of the news story and also claimed that US government is trying to cover-up human rights abuse and other criminal behaviour (The Moscow Times, 2010). Meanwhile, this story in The Moscow Times also categorically cherry picked those British and US newspapers which carried the leaks and are critical of the US in their reporting.

In an opinion piece for The Moscow Times penned by Harold Evans, British journalist and former editor of The Sunday Times newspaper, maintained that publishing such classified documents is highly detrimental in nature (2010). In the article titled 'Right to print wiki cables,' he went to assert that what WikiLeaks has been doing is not journalism and also criticised the newspapers who published WikiLeaks' data stating, "Any editor with pretensions to responsible journalism must hesitate over publishing the WikiLeaks' cache of U.S. diplomatic cables raw" (The Moscow Times, 2010). "How should we judge the WikiLeaks dumpings and more to follow? How far do they pass the test of good journalism?" he questioned (The Moscow Times, 2010).

A 2013 news story published on the Russia Today website which reported about a leaked confidential letter of the UK cabinet that urged the MPs to refrain from discussing the 2003 Iraq invasion or its legality until an inquiry into it is complete. This same news story also mentioned about the Iraq war leaks stating, 'the WikiLeaks Iraq war logs showed that more than 90,000 Iraqi civilians died throughout the course of the conflict, placing the overall number of Iraqi deaths at over 100,000' (Russia Today, 2013). It further said, 'the 2003 invasion resulted in the deaths of tens of thousands of Iraqis, and 179 British deaths.'

Interestingly, while emphasis was put on the death of Iraqis who are referred as 'civilians,' the number of British causalities were shown as only 179 compared to 100,000 Iraqi deaths.

Furthermore, this story put an in-depth account of people's disapproval towards Britain supporting the war. Eliciting that the report mentions about a protest demonstration of February 2003 when an estimated 750,000 to 1-million-plus protesters participated in anti-war demonstrations; the march in London was named the largest political demonstration Britain had ever seen (Russia Today, 2010).

Another news story featured by the Russia Today website while reporting on a book titled 'The Wikileaks Files,' authored by Jullian Assange, called the killings revealed in Iraq War logs as 'extra judicial killings' (2015).

Conclusion

Analysing the reporting of Iraq War logs in Indian newspapers, the line that was adopted is seen to be quite mixed. Majority of the news stories analysed, were found to hold a soft approach for WikiLeaks and were seen as critical of both the Iraq war and hounding of Jullian Assange by US authorities after WikiLeaks published the Iraq war logs. However, few newspapers or news stories were also seen to be critical of Assange and his type of journalism. But, it can be discerned that India's good diplomatic terms with the US and UK could not have much influence on how newspapers reported the Iraq war leaks episode. Mostly Indian media was seen to have been lenient towards WikiLeaks while reporting.

This mixed response very well gels up with the nature of Indian journalism. As one of the author argues, 'the front pages of mainstream Indian newspapers veer between celebrity-mongering and reports on Indian tycoons, beauty queens, filmmakers, and other achievers in the West' (Rao, 474). Though at a superficial level, but press freedom exists in India to a large extent. Therefore, according to Rao media landscape, despite having been made possible by globalization and configured by pro-market logic, has created the opportunity for a journalism of 'janapakshi' (pro-people) to evolve. It has fundamentally reconfigured the relationship between the journalist and the reader/viewer as a democratic and equitable one (Rao, 486).

Shifting focus to Russian media, the news reporting was found to be anti-UK/US. Lines could easily be drawn with Russia's anti-war stance and also the media was seen to be supportive of the state's voice. Unlike in Indian newspapers where different views were espied in regards to WikiLeaks, in Russian media apart from opinion pieces the news space was very much critical of the US's policies and portrayed WikiLeaks and Jullian Assange as a crusader of free speech. Added to that the nature of Russian media being pro-government could also be seen as a reason why there lacked a dissident voice.

As one writer explains Russia experienced the emergence of media empires and information wars during which political and economic groups fought one another in the media, mainly television (Pietiläinen, 365).

It could be seen from the discourse analysis that Russia Today being a government run media outlet, it is very obvious to package news supporting the policies of the state and weave its news coverage in line of the state voice. However, the same course of reporting was seen by other newspapers including The Moscow Time and Moscow News as well.

The reason could also be seen as Putin's presidency with public support, increased the control of the state over national television. In newspapers and at regional level, political and economic sponsorship and a wide spectrum of diversity have remained and in the present context the media have changed from being 'spokespeople for democratic change to tools in internal power struggles among the political and business elite' and have reverted to the role they played under Soviet rule: the government's propaganda machine (Pietiläinen, 366).

Bibliography

1) "Ex-Australian PM Embarrassed by 2003 Iraq Invasion." Indo-Asian News Service. 22 Sept. 2014. Web. 29 Dec. 2015.

2) "The Crisis of Conscience." Kashmir Monitor 9 Aug. 2011. Web. 29 Dec. 2015.

3) Sinha, Kounteya. "Barman Tries to 'arrest' Blair for Iraq War Crimes." The Times of India 23 Jan. 2014, UK sec. Web. 29 Dec. 2015.

4) Nikolaev, Alexander G. *Leading to the 2003 Iraq War the Global Media Debate*. New York: Palgrave Macmillan, 2006. Print.

5) Zolotov Jr, Andrei. "A Bias Ekes Out Of War Coverage." The Moscow Times 2 Apr. 2003. Web. 30 Dec. 2015.

6) "Britain's Blair Says 2003 Iraq Invasion Played Role in Islamic State Rise." *Moscow News* 25 Oct. 2015. Web. 30 Dec. 2015.

7) "The Links between the UK and India." *BBC News*. BBC, 12 Nov. 2015. Web. 30 Dec. 2015.

8) Coyle Emer, Mona Lotten, and John Dubber. "INDIA MATTERS How Stronger Educational and Cultural Ties Can Help to Unlock the Full Potential of the UK–India Relationship." *British Council* (2015): 17- 28. *British Council*. British Council. Web. 30 Dec. 2015.

9) Owen, Jonathan. "UK-India Relations: 'Colonial Mindset' Harming British Trade with India." *Independent* 27 Oct. 2015, Home News sec. Web. 30 Dec. 2015.

10) Rowlatt, Justin. "Modi Visit: UK and India's 'special Relationship' Hailed." *BBC News*. BBC, 13 Nov. 2015. Web. 30 Dec. 2015. <http://www.bbc.co.uk/news/uk-34806511>.

11) "What's in WikiLeaks' Iraq War Logs?" *Hindustan Times* 23 Oct. 2010. HT Media. Web. 30 Dec. 2015.

12) "Don't Shooot the Messenger: Assange." *The Times of India* 9 Dec. 2010. Bennett Coleman & Co. Ltd. Web. 30 Dec. 2015.

13) "Hidden World of US Diplomacy Exposed." *Kashmir Observer* 29 Nov. 2010. Web. 31 Dec. 2015.

14) Mehta, Neha Tara. "Former Wiki Member Takes on Assange." *Mail Today* 11 Dec. 2010, Delhi ed. The India Today Group. Web. 31 Dec. 2015.

15) "Mail Today among Rs 211.66-cr FDI Plans Cleared." *The Hindu* 3 Nov. 2007, Business Line sec. N Ram. Web. 31 Dec. 2015.

16) "India Today Group to Launch Tabloid in Partnership with Daily Mail." *Live Mint* 13 Nov. 2007. Vivk Khanna. Web. 31 Dec. 2015.

17) Mahapatra, Chintamani. "India–US Ties: Reviewing the Relationship." *Strategic Analysis* 39. February (2015): 170-75. Print.

18) Stent, Angela. "US–Russia Relations in the Second Obama Administration." *Survival* 54.6, 2012 (2012): 123-38. Print.

19) David, Maxine. "A Less than Special Relationship: The UK's Russia Experience." *Journal of Contemporary European Studies* 19.2, 2011 (2011): 201-12. Print.

20) Dathan, Matt. "Vladimir Putin: Paris Attacks Triggered a 'revival' in Russia-UK Relations." *Independent* 16 Nov. 2015, UK Politics sec. Independent Print Limited. Web. 2016.

21) Latynina, Yulia. "WikiLeaks Is Fighting the Wrong Enemy." *The Moscow Times* 24 Nov. 2010, Opinion sec. Moscow Times LLC. Web. 2016.

22) "WikiLeaks Publishes U.S. Diplomatic Cables." *The Moscow Times* 29 Nov. 2010, News sec. Moscow Times LLC. Web. 2016.

23) Evans, Harold. "Right to Print Wiki Cables." *The Moscow Times* 6 Dec. 2010, Opinion sec. Moscow Times LLC. Web. 2016.

24) "UK FM Hague Instructed Cabinet Not to Mention Iraq War – Report." *Russia Today*. Russian Government, 1 Mar. 2013. Web. 2016. <https://www.rt.com/news/iraq-hague-leak-anniversary-655/>.

25) "Julian Assange: 'Snowden, I and Kim Dotcom All Assigned Same Prosecutor in Virginia'." *Russia Today*. Russian Government, 8 Oct. 2015. Web. 2016. <https://www.rt.com/news/318000-assange-interview-snowden-dotcom/>.

26) Rao, Shakuntala. "Glocalization Of Indian Journalism." *Journalism Studies* 10.4, 2009 (2009): 474-88. Print.

27) Pietiläinen, Jukka. "Media Use in Putin's Russia." *Journal of Communist Studies and Transition Politics* 24.3, 2008 (2008): 365-85. Print.

28) Brevini, Benedetta, Patrick McCurdy, and Arne Hintz. *Beyond WikiLeaks Implications for the Future of*

Communications, Journalism and Society. Basingstoke: Palgrave Macmillan, 2013. Print.

29) "What Is WikiLeaks." *What Is WikiLeaks.* 3 Nov. 2015. Web. 9 Jan. 2016.

30) Romaya, Bassam. *The Iraq War: A Philosophical Analysis.* New York: Palgrave Macmillan, 2012. Print.

31) Danju, Ipek, Yasar Maasoglu, and Nahide Maasoglu. "The Reasons Behind U.S. Invasion of Iraq." *Procedia - Social and Behavioral Sciences* (2013): 682-90. Print.

32) "Iraq War Logs Reveal 15,000 Previously Unlisted Civilian Deaths." *The Guardian* 22 Oct. 2010, World sec. Guardian News and Media. Web. 9 Jan. 2016.

Leaks, WikiLeaks and the Press